Noises
in the Night

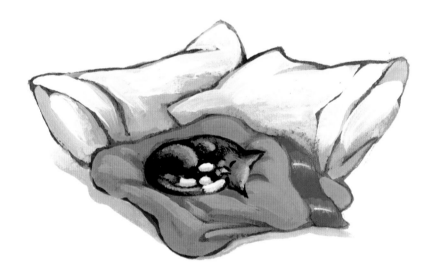

Pam Zollman
Illustrated by Stacey Schuett

Rigby.

"Catch!" Clara tossed pillows at
Silvia and Lourdes, who were spending
the night.

Clara's mother walked into the living
room and gave each girl a flashlight.
"You can use these if you have to get
up in the middle of the night."

    Clara's cat Luna rubbed against
Mom's leg. "I didn't forget you," Mom
said as she tossed her a little ball. Luna
looked at it, flicked her tail, and then
walked away.

    "Luna may not like her present," Clara
said, "but we love our presents!"

The girls finished getting ready for bed. Then they stretched out on the living room floor with their pillows and blankets.

As soon as Clara turned out the light, Lourdes whispered, "Let's tell scary stories."

Sitting up, Clara put her glasses back on and said, "I know a good story."

"Is it really scary?" Silvia asked. "Does it have monsters in it?"

Clara giggled and said, "This story is about a girl alone in the house at night. Then there's a bad storm and all of the lights go out. Suddenly she hears a strange noise."

A jingling noise rang through the living room, and Clara stopped talking.

"Clara, are you trying to scare us?"
Lourdes asked.

"No, it wasn't me," Clara said. The
friends moved closer together. They heard
the jingling noise again, so Clara turned
on her flashlight.

"I think it came from the hallway,"
Silvia said, shivering.

Lourdes turned on her flashlight and said, "Let's go see what it is."

The light from their flashlights made creepy shadows across the walls as they walked down the hall.

"Maybe it was Mom," Clara whispered.

They peeked into her mother's room, but Mom was asleep. They heard the jingling noise again, but this time it came from the living room. The three girls walked back down the hallway.

Suddenly Silvia grabbed Clara's arm and said, "Did you see that shadow move?"

"Someone or something is out there," Lourdes whispered.

"Mom is asleep, and there's no one else here."

"Maybe it's a monster," Silvia said. She turned off her flashlight. "I don't want the monster to see me."

They heard the jingling noise again, and they could hear something running across the living room.

"That shadow looks like a monster!"
cried Lourdes.

"It's making a scratching sound,"
said Silvia.

Clara giggled nervously and said,
"A tree branch is rubbing against
the window."

Just then the jingling noise came closer,
and Silvia screamed, "Watch out!
Something touched me. It was a
hairy monster!"

They heard the jingling noise at their feet. Clara turned on the lamp and the three girls started laughing. Luna looked up at them.

"I heard someone scream," said Mom sleepily from the hallway.

"We thought a hairy monster was in the room with us," said Lourdes.

Clara pointed to her cat, who was hitting a jingling ball around the room. "Luna was the hairy monster. She likes her present now."

As the girls laid on their blankets
blankets again, Silvia whispered,
"No more scary stories."

"No more scary noises,"
Lourdes added.

Suddenly there was a loud purring
noise in the darkness, and the three
girls laughed.

Clara petted her purring cat and said,
"This is the night noise I like best."